Sleeping Beauties

USA

ABANDONED CLASSIC CARS & TRUCKS

Other great books from Veloce –

Speedpro Series
4-cylinder Engine – How to Blueprint & Build a Short Block For High Performance (Hammill)
Alfa Romeo DOHC High-performance Manual (Kartalamakis)
Alfa Romeo V6 Engine High-performance Manual (Kartalamakis)
BMC 998cc A-series Engine – How to Power Tune (Hammill)
1275cc A-series High-performance Manual (Hammill)
Camshafts – How to Choose & Time Them For Maximum Power (Hammill)
Competition Car Datalogging Manual, The (Templeman)
Cylinder Heads – How to Build, Modify & Power Tune Updated & Revised Edition (Burgess & Gollan)
Distributor-type Ignition Systems – How to Build & Power Tune New 3rd Edition (Hammill)
Fast Road Car – How to Plan and Build Revised & Updated Colour New Edition (Stapleton)
Ford SOHC 'Pinto' & Sierra Cosworth DOHC Engines – How to Power Tune Updated & Enlarged Edition (Hammill)
Ford V8 – How to Power Tune Small Block Engines (Hammill)
Harley-Davidson Evolution Engines – How to Build & Power Tune (Hammill)
Holley Carburetors – How to Build & Power Tune Revised & Updated Edition (Hammill)
Honda Civic Type R, The – High-Performance Manual (Cowland & Clifford)
Jaguar XK Engines – How to Power Tune Revised & Updated Colour Edition (Hammill)
Land Rover Discovery, Defender & Range Rover – How to Modify Coil Sprung Models for High Performance & Off-Road Action (Hosier)
MG Midget & Austin-Healey Sprite – How to Power Tune New 3rd Edition (Stapleton)
MGB 4-cylinder Engine – How to Power Tune (Burgess)
MGB V8 Power – How to Give Your, Third Colour Edition (Williams)
MGB, MGC & MGB V8 – How to Improve New 2nd Edition (Williams)
Mini Engines – How to Power Tune On a Small Budget Colour Edition (Hammill)
Motorcycle-engined Racing Car – How to Build (Pashley)
Motorsport – Getting Started in (Collins)
Nissan GT-R High-performance Manual, The (Gorodji)
Nitrous Oxide High-performance Manual, The (Langfield)
Rover V8 Engines – How to Power Tune (Hammill)
Secrets of Speed – Today's techniques for 4-stroke engine blueprinting & tuning (Swager)
Sportscar & Kitcar Suspension & Brakes – How to Build & Modify Revised 3rd Edition (Hammill)
SU Carburettor High-performance Manual (Hammill)
Successful Low-Cost Rally Car, How to Build a (Young)
Suzuki 4x4 – How to Modify For Serious Off-road Action (Richardson)
Tiger Avon Sportscar – How to Build Your Own Updated & Revised 2nd Edition (Dudley)
TR2, 3 & TR4 – How to Improve (Williams)
TR5, 250 & TR6 – How to Improve (Williams)
TR7 & TR8 – How to Improve (Williams)
V8 Engine – How to Build a Short Block For High Performance (Hammill)
Volkswagen Beetle Suspension, Brakes & Chassis – How to Modify For High Performance (Hale)
Volkswagen Bus Suspension, Brakes & Chassis – How to Modify For High Performance (Hale)
Weber DCOE, & Dellorto DHLA Carburetors – How to Build & Power Tune 3rd Edition (Hammill)

Those Were The Days ... Series
Alpine Trials & Rallies 1910-1973 (Pfundner)
American 'Independent' Automakers – AMC to Willys 1945 to 1960 (Mort)
American Station Wagons – The Golden Era 1950-1975 (Mort)
American Trucks of the 1950s (Mort)
American Trucks of the 1960s (Mort)
American Woodies 1928-1953 (Mort)
Anglo-American Cars from the 1930s to the 1970s (Mort)
Austerity Motoring (Bobbitt)
Austins, The last real (Peck)
Brighton National Speed Trials (Gardiner)
British Lorries of the 1950s (Bobbitt)
British Lorries of the 1960s (Bobbitt)
British Touring Car Racing (Collins)
British Police Cars (Walker)
British Woodies (Peck)
Café Racer Phenomenon, The (Walker)
Drag Bike Racing in Britain – From the mid '60s to the mid '80s (Lee)
Dune Buggy Phenomenon, The (Hale)
Dune Buggy Phenomenon Volume 2, The (Hale)
Endurance Racing at Silverstone in the 1970s & 1980s (Parker)
Hot Rod & Stock Car Racing in Britain in the 1980s (Neil)
Last Real Austins 1946-1959, The (Peck)
MG's Abingdon Factory (Moylan)
Motor Racing at Brands Hatch in the Seventies (Parker)
Motor Racing at Brands Hatch in the Eighties (Parker)
Motor Racing at Crystal Palace (Collins)
Motor Racing at Goodwood in the Sixties (Gardiner)
Motor Racing at Nassau in the 1950s & 1960s (O'Neil)
Motor Racing at Oulton Park in the 1960s (McFadyen)
Motor Racing at Oulton Park in the 1970s (McFadyen)
Superprix – The Story of Birmingham Motor Race (Page & Collins)
Three Wheelers (Bobbitt)

Truckmakers
DAF Trucks since 1949 (Peck)

Enthusiast's Restoration Manual Series
Citroën 2CV, How to Restore (Porter)
Classic Car Bodywork, How to Restore (Thaddeus)
Classic British Car Electrical Systems (Astley)
Classic Car Electrics (Thaddeus)
Classic Cars, How to Paint (Thaddeus)
Reliant Regal, How to Restore (Payne)
Triumph TR2, 3, 3A, 4 & 4A, How to Restore (Williams)
Triumph TR5/250 & 6, How to Restore (Williams)
Triumph TR7/8, How to Restore (Williams)
Volkswagen Beetle, How to Restore (Tyler)
VW Bay Window Bus (Paxton)
Yamaha FS1-E, How to Restore (Watts)

Essential Buyer's Guide Series
Alfa GT (Booker)
Alfa Romeo Spider Giulia (Booker & Talbott)
Austin Seven (Barker)
BMW GS (Henshaw)
BSA Bantam (Henshaw)
BSA 500 & 650 Twins (Henshaw)
Citroën 2CV (Paxton)
Citroën ID & DS (Heilig)
Corvette C2 1963-1967 (Falconer)
Fiat 500 & 600 (Bobbitt)
Ford Capri (Paxton)
Harley-Davidson Big Twins (Henshaw)
Hinckley Triumph triples & fours 750, 900, 955, 1000, 1050, 1200 – 1991-2009 (Henshaw)
Honda CBR600 (Henshaw)
Honda FireBlade (Henshaw)
Honda SOHC fours 1969-1984 (Henshaw)
Jaguar E-type 3.8 & 4.2-litre (Crespin)
Jaguar E-type V12 5.3-litre (Crespin)
Jaguar XJ 1995-2003 (Crespin)
Jaguar/Daimler XJ6, XJ12 & Sovereign (Crespin)
Jaguar/Daimler XJ40 (Crespin)
Jaguar XJ-S (Crespin)
Land Rover Series I, II & IIA (Thurman)
MGB & MGB GT (Williams)
Mercedes-Benz 280SL-560DSL Roadsters (Bass)
Mercedes-Benz 'Pagoda' 230SL, 250SL & 280SL Roadsters & Coupés (Bass)
MG Midget & A-H Sprite (Horler)
MG TD, TF & TF1500 (Jones)
Mini (Paxton)
Morris Minor & 1000 (Newell)
Norton Commando (Henshaw)
Peugeot 205 GTi (Blackburn)
Porsche 911 (964) (Streather)
Porsche 911 (993) (Streather)
Porsche 911 (996) (Streather)
Porsche 911 SC (Streather)
Porsche 928 (Hemmings)
Rolls-Royce Silver Shadow & Bentley T-Series (Bobbitt)
Subaru Impreza (Hobbs)
Triumph Bonneville (Henshaw)
Triumph Spitfire & GT6
Triumph Stag (Mort & Fox)
Triumph TR6 (Williams)
Triumph TR7 & TR8 (Williams)
Vespa Scooters – Classic 2-stroke models 1960-2008 (Paxton)
VW Beetle (Cservenka & Copping)
VW Bus (Cservenka & Copping)
VW Golf GTI (Cservenka & Copping)

Auto-Graphics Series
Fiat-based Abarths (Sparrow)
Jaguar MKI & II Saloons (Sparrow)
Lambretta Li Series Scooters (Sparrow)

Rally Giants Series
Audi Quattro (Robson)
Austin Healey 100-6 & 3000 (Robson)
Fiat 131 Abarth (Robson)
Ford Escort MkI (Robson)
Ford Escort RS Cosworth & World Rally Car (Robson)
Ford Escort RS1800 (Robson)
Lancia Delta 4WD/Integrale (Robson)
Lancia Stratos (Robson)
Mini Cooper/Mini Cooper S (Robson)
Peugeot 205 T16 (Robson)
Saab 96 & V4 (Robson)
Subaru Impreza (Robson)
Toyota Celica GT4 (Robson)

WSC Giants
Ferrari 312P & 312PB (Collins & McDonough)
Gulf-Mirage 1967 to 1982 (McDonough)
Matra Sports Cars – MS620, 630, 650, 660 & 670 – 1966 to 1974 (McDonough)

General
1½-litre GP Racing 1961-1965 (Whitelock)
AC Two-litre Saloons & Buckland Sportscars (Archibald)
Alfa Romeo Giulia Coupé GT & GTA (Tipler)
Alfa Romeo Montreal – The dream car that came true (Taylor)
Alfa Romeo Montreal – The Essential Companion (Taylor)
Alfa Tipo 33 (McDonough & Collins)
Alpine & Renault – The Development of the Revolutionary Turbo F1 Car 1968 to 1979 (Smith)
Alpine & Renault – The Sports Prototypes 1963 to 1969 (Smith)
Alpine & Renault – The Sports Prototypes 1973 to 1978 (Smith)
Anatomy of the Works Minis (Moylan)
André Lefebvre, and the cars he created at Voisin and Citroën (Beck)
Armstrong-Siddeley (Smith)
Art Deco and British Car Design (Down)
Autodrome (Collins & Ireland)
Autodrome 2 (Collins & Ireland)
Automotive A-Z, Lane's Dictionary of Automotive Terms (Lane)
Automotive Mascots (Kay & Springate)
Bahamas Speed Weeks, The (O'Neil)
Bentley Continental, Corniche and Azure (Bennett)
Bentley MkVI, Rolls-Royce Silver Wraith, Dawn & Cloud/Bentley R & S-Series (Nutland)
Bluebird CN7 (Stevens)
BMC Competitions Department Secrets (Turner, Chambers & Browning)
BMW 5-Series (Cranswick)
BMW Z-Cars (Taylor)
BMW Boxer Twins 1970-1995 Bible, The (Falloon)
Britains Farm Model Balers & Combines 1967-2007, Pocket Guide to (Pullen)
Britains Farm Model & Toy Tractors 1998-2008, Pocket Guide to (Pullen)
Britains Toy Models Catalogues 1970-1979 (Pullen)
British 250cc Racing Motorcycles (Pereira)
British at Indianapolis, The (Wagstaff)
British Cars, The Complete Catalogue of, 1895-1975 (Culshaw & Horrobin)
BRM – A Mechanic's Tale (Salmon)
BRM V16 (Ludvigsen)
BSA Bantam Bible, The (Henshaw)
Bugatti Type 40 (Price)
Bugatti 46/50 Updated Edition (Price & Arbey)
Bugatti T44 & T49 (Price & Arbey)
Bugatti 57 2nd Edition (Price)
Caravans, The Illustrated History 1919-1959 (Jenkinson)
Caravans, The Illustrated History From 1960 (Jenkinson)
Carrera Panamericana, La (Tipler)
Chrysler 300 – America's Most Powerful Car 2nd Edition (Ackerson)
Chrysler PT Cruiser (Ackerson)
Citroën DS (Bobbitt)
Classic British Car Electrical Systems (Astley)
Cliff Allison, The Official Biography of – From the Fells to Ferrari – (Gauld)
Cobra – The Real Thing! (Legate)
Concept Cars, How to illustrate and design (Dewey)
Cortina – Ford's Bestseller (Robson)
Coventry Climax Racing Engines (Hammill)
Daily Mirror 1970 World Cup Rally 40, The (Robson)
Daimler SP250 New Edition (Long)
Datsun Fairlady Roadster to 280ZX – The Z-Car Story (Long)
Diecast Toy Cars of the 1950s & 1960s (Ralston)
Dino – The V6 Ferrari (Long)
Dodge Challenger & Plymouth Barracuda (Grist)
Dodge Charger – Enduring Thunder (Ackerson)
Dodge Dynamite! (Grist)
Draw & Paint Cars – How to (Gardiner)
Drive on the Wild Side, A – 20 Extreme Driving Adventures From Around the World (Weaver)
Ducati 750 Bible, The (Falloon)
Ducati 750 SS 'round-case' 1974, The Book of the (Falloon)
Ducati 860, 900 and Mille Bible, The (Falloon)
Dune Buggy, Building A – The Essential Manual (Shakespeare)
Dune Buggy Files (Hale)
Dune Buggy Handbook (Hale)
East German Motor Vehicles in Pictures (Suhr/Weinreich)
Edward Turner: The Man Behind the Motorcycles (Clew)
Efficient Driver's Handbook, The (Moss)
Electric Cars – The Future is Now! (Linde)
Fast Ladies – Female Racing Drivers 1888 to 1970 (Bouzanquet)
Fate of the Sleeping Beauties, The (op de Weegh/Hottendorff/op de Weegh)
Ferrari 288 GTO, The Book of the (Sackey)
Fiat & Abarth 124 Spider & Coupé (Tipler)
Fiat & Abarth 500 & 600 2nd Edition (Bobbitt)
Fiats, Great Small (Ward)
Fine Art of the Motorcycle Engine, The (Peirce)
Ford F100/F150 Pick-up 1948-1996 (Ackerson)
Ford F150 Pick-up 1997-2005 (Ackerson)
Ford GT – Then, and Now (Streather)
Ford GT40 (Legate)
Ford In Miniature (Olson)
Ford Model Y (Roberts)
Ford Thunderbird From 1954, The Book of the (Long)
Formula 5000 Motor Racing, Back then ... and back now (Lawson)
Forza Minardi! (Vigar)
Funky Mopeds (Skelton)
GM In Miniature (Olson)
GT – The World's Best GT Cars 1953-73 (Dawson)
Hillclimbing & Sprinting – The Essential Manual (Short & Wilkinson)
Honda NSX (Long)
Intermeccanica – The Story of the Prancing Bull (McCredie & Reisner)
Jack Sears, The Official Biography of – Gentleman Jack (Gauld)
Jaguar, The Rise of (Price)
Jaguar XJ 220 – The Inside Story (Moreton)
Jaguar XJ-S (Long)
Jeep CJ (Ackerson)
Jeep Wrangler (Ackerson)
John Chatham – 'Mr Big Healey' – The Official Biography (Burr)
Karmann-Ghia Coupé & Convertible (Bobbitt)
Kawasaki Triples Bible, The (Walker)
Kris Meeke – Intercontinental Rally Challenge Champion (McBride)
Lamborghini Miura Bible, The (Sackey)
Lamborghini Urraco, The book of the (Landsem)
Lambretta Bible, The (Davies)
Lancia 037 (Collins)
Lancia Delta HF Integrale (Blaettel & Wagner)
Land Rover Series III Reborn (Porter)
Land Rover, The Half-ton Military (Cook)
Laverda Twins & Triples Bible 1968-1986 (Falloon)
Lea-Francis Story, The (Price)
Lexus Story, The (Long)
little book of smart, the New Edition (Jackson)
little book of microcars, the (Quellin)
Lola – The Illustrated History (1957-1977) (Starkey)
Lola – All the Sports Racing & Single-seater Racing Cars 1978-1997 (Starkey)
Lola T70 – The Racing History & Individual Chassis Record 4th Edition (Starkey)
Lotus 49 (Oliver)
Marketingmobiles, The Wonderful Wacky World of (Hale)
Mazda MX-5/Miata 1.6 Enthusiast's Workshop Manual (Grainger & Shoemark)
Mazda MX-5/Miata 1.8 Enthusiast's Workshop Manual (Grainger & Shoemark)
Mazda MX-5 Miata: The Book of the World's Favourite Sportscar (Long)
Mazda MX-5 Miata Roadster (Long)
Maximum Mini (Booij)
Mercedes-Benz SL – 113-series 1963-1971 (Long)
Mercedes-Benz SL & SLC – 107-series 1971-1989 (Long)
MGA (Price Williams)
MGB & MGB GT– Expert Guide (Auto-doc Series) (Williams)
MGB Electrical Systems Updated & Revised Edition (Astley)
Micro Caravans (Jenkinson)
Micro Trucks (Mort)
Microcars at Large! (Quellin)
Mini Cooper – The Real Thing! (Tipler)
Mitsubishi Lancer Evo, The Road Car & WRC Story (Long)
Montlhéry, The Story of the Paris Autodrome (Boddy)
Morgan Maverick (Lawrence)
Morris Minor, 60 Years on the Road (Newell)
Moto Guzzi Sport & Le Mans Bible, The (Falloon)
Motor Movies – The Posters! (Veysey)
Motor Racing – Reflections of a Lost Era (Carter)
Motorcycle Apprentice (Cakebread)
Motorcycle Road & Racing Chassis Designs (Noakes)
Motorhomes, The Illustrated History (Jenkinson)
Motorsport In colour, 1950s (Wainwright)
Nissan 300ZX & 350Z – The Z-Car Story (Long)
Nissan GT-R Supercar: Born to race (Gorodji)
Northeast American Sports Car Races 1950-1959 (O'Neil)
Off-Road Giants! – Heroes of 1960s Motorcycle Sport (Westlake)
Pass the Theory and Practical Driving Tests (Gibson & Hoole)
Pat Moss Carlsson Story, The – Harnessing Horsepower (Turner)
Peking to Paris 2007 (Young)
Plastic Toy Cars of the 1950s & 1960s (Ralston)
Pontiac Firebird (Cranswick)
Porsche Boxster (Long)
Porsche 356 (2nd Edition) (Long)
Porsche 908 (Födisch, Neßhöver, Roßbach, Schwarz & Roßbach)
Porsche 911 Carrera – The Last of the Evolution (Corlett)
Porsche 911R, RS & RSR, 4th Edition (Starkey)
Porsche 911, The Book of the (Long)
Porsche 911 – The Definitive History 1963-1971 (Long)
Porsche 911 – The Definitive History 1971-1977 (Long)
Porsche 911 – The Definitive History 1977-1987 (Long)
Porsche 911 – The Definitive History 1987-1997 (Long)
Porsche 911 – The Definitive History 1997-2004 (Long)
Porsche 911SC 'Super Carrera' – The Essential Companion (Streather)
Porsche 914 & 914-6: The Definitive History of the Road & Competition Cars (Long)
Porsche 924 (Long)
Porsche 928 (Long)
Porsche 944 (Long)
Porsche 964, 993 & 996 Data Plate Code Breaker (Streather)
Porsche 993 'King Of Porsche' – The Essential Companion (Streather)
Porsche 996 'Supreme Porsche' – The Essential Companion (Streather)
Porsche Racing Cars – 1953 to 1975 (Long)
Porsche Racing Cars – 1976 to 2005 (Long)
Porsche – The Rally Story (Meredith)
Porsche: Three Generations of Genius (Meredith)
Preston Tucker & Others (Linde)
RAC Rally Action! (Gardiner)
Rallye Sport Fords: The Inside Story (Moreton)
Redman, Jim – 6 Times World Motorcycle Champion: The Autobiography (Redman)
Roads with a View – England's greatest views and how to find them by road (Corfield)
Rolls-Royce Silver Shadow/Bentley T Series Corniche & Camargue Revised & Enlarged Edition (Bobbitt)
Rolls-Royce Silver Spirit, Silver Spur & Bentley Mulsanne 2nd Edition (Bobbitt)
Runways & Racers (O'Neil)
Russian Motor Vehicles – Soviet Limousines 1930-2003 (Kelly)
Russian Motor Vehicles – The Czarist Period 1784 to 1917 (Kelly)
RX-7 – Mazda's Rotary Engine Sportscar (Updated & Revised New Edition) (Long)
Scooters & Microcars, The A-Z of Popular (Dan)
Scooter Lifestyle (Grainger)
Singer Story: Cars, Commercial Vehicles, Bicycles & Motorcycle (Atkinson)
Sleeping Beauties USA – abandoned classic cars & trucks (Marek)
SM – Citroën's Maserati-engined Supercar (Long & Claverol)
Speedway – Auto racing's ghost tracks (Collins & Ireland)
Subaru Impreza: The Road Car And WRC Story (Long)
Supercar, How to Build your own (Thompson)
Tales from the Toolbox (Oliver)
Taxi! The Story of the 'London' Taxicab (Bobbitt)
Tinplate Toy Cars of the 1950s & 1960s (Ralston)
Toleman Story, The (Hilton)
Toyota Celica & Supra, The Book of Toyota's Sports Coupés (Long)
Toyota MR2 Coupés & Spyders (Long)
Triumph Bonneville!, Save the – The inside story of the Meriden Workers' Co-op (Rosamond)
Triumph Motorcycles & the Meriden Factory (Hancox)
Triumph Speed Twin & Thunderbird Bible (Woolridge)
Triumph Tiger Cub Bible (Estall)
Triumph Trophy Bible (Woolridge)
Triumph TR6 (Kimberley)
TWR Story, The – Group A (Hughes & Scott)
Unraced (Collins)
Velocette Motorcycles – MSS to Thruxton New Third Edition (Burris)
Virgil Exner – Visioneer: The Official Biography of Virgil M Exner Designer Extraordinaire (Grist)
Volkswagen Bus Book, The (Bobbitt)
Volkswagen Bus or Van to Camper, How to Convert (Porter)
Volkswagens of the World (Glen)
VW Beetle Cabriolet (Bobbitt)
VW Beetle – The Car of the 20th Century (Copping)
VW Bus – 40 Years of Splitties, Bays & Wedges (Copping)
VW Bus Book, The (Bobbitt)
VW Golf: Five Generations of Fun (Copping & Cservenka)
VW – The Air-cooled Era (Copping)
VW T5 Camper Conversion Manual (Porter)
VW Campers (Copping)
Works Minis, The Last (Purves & Brenchley)
Works Rally Mechanic (Moylan)

From Veloce Publishing's new imprints:

Battle Cry!
Soviet General & field rank officer uniforms: 1955 to 1991 (Streather)
Red & Soviet military & paramilitary services: female uniforms 1941-1991 (Streather)

Hubble & Hattie
Clever Dog! (O'Meara)
Complete Dog Massage Manual, The – Gentle Dog Care (Robertson)
Dinner with Rover (Paton-Ayre)
Dog Cookies (Schops)
Dog Games – Stimulating play to entertain your dog and you (Blenski)
Dogs on wheels (Mort)
Dog Relax – Relaxed dogs, relaxed owners (Pilguj)
Exercising your puppy: a gentle & natural approach (Robertson)
Know Your Dog – The guide to a beautiful relationship (Birmelin)
Living with an Older Dog (Alderton & Hall)
My dog has cruciate ligament injury (Häusler)
My dog has hip dysplasia (Häusler)
My dog is blind – but lives life to the full! (Horsky)
My dog is deaf (Willms)
Smellorama – nose games for dogs (Theby)
Swim to Recovery: Canine hydrotherapy healing (Wong)
Waggy Tails & Wheelchairs (Epp)
Walkin' the dog – motorway walks for drivers and dogs (Rees)
Winston ... the dog who changed my life (Klute)
You and Your Border Terrier – The Essential Guide (Alderton)
You and Your Cockapoo – The Essential Guide (Alderton)
You and Your Cockapoo – The Essential Guide (Alderton)

www.velocebooks.com

First published in November 2010 by Veloce Publishing Limited, Veloce House, Parkway Farm Business Park, Middle Farm Way, Poundbury, Dorchester, Dorset, DT1 3AR, England.
Fax 01305 250479/e-mail info@veloce.co.uk/web www.veloce.co.uk or www.velocebooks.com.

ISBN: 978-1-845843-46-5 UPC: 6-36847-04346-9

British Library Cataloguing in Publication Data – A catalogue record for this book is available from the British Library. Typesetting, design and page make-up all by Veloce Publishing Ltd on Apple Mac. Printed in India by Imprint Digital.

Sleeping Beauties USA

USA

ABANDONED CLASSIC CARS & TRUCKS

VELOCE PUBLISHING
THE PUBLISHER OF FINE AUTOMOTIVE BOOKS

Contents

Introduction. 5

Field of dreams 6
Forgotten luxury.. 8
Thunderbird relic 10
Forgotten Mopar. 12
Ghost 15
Shrunken truck 16
Rare-muscle Mopar. 19
Fifties survivor. 20
Lost Comet 22
Firemen's favourite 25
Luxury beside the road 26
International workhorse. .. .. .29
Stylish ambulance .. .. .31
German duo. .. .. .32
Entry-level elegance 34
For the family 36
Forgotten four .. .. .39
Postwar premiere 40
A fallen meteor .. .. .43
Old giant.. 44
Big hauler .. .. .47
Nature is calling.. .. .. .49

Family truck. .. .. .50
Apache pickup. .. .. .52
Group picture of the generations.. .. .. .54
Hay transporter .. .. .56
Classic duo .. .. .58
Historic stop .. .. .60
Prewar truck .. .. .62
School's out. 64
Route 66 commemoration .. .. .. .66
Ghost town relic.. .. .. .68
Super Sedan .. .. .71
Pickup mania .. .. .73
Fine Forties.. .. .. .74
Back to the Eighties .. .. .77
Studebaker graveyard 78
Old survivor. 80
Rusty companion .. .. .83
Studebaker's workhorse .. .. .85
Postwar child 87
Eager beaver 88
Batwings.. .. .. .90

Index .. .. .96

Introduction

This book, *Sleeping Beauties USA,* honors rusted and forgotten automotive treasures that have been found parked alongside the highways of America, waiting to be rediscovered.

Rather than focusing on typically brilliant, highly restored show queens, I have instead concentrated on showing, through stunning and evocative photography, the transience of a car's life and the beauty created as nature reclaims her own. I hope the pictures will give you as much pleasure as I enjoyed when I first saw the cars and trucks in reality and reminisced about their once glorious past.

At this point, I would also like to thank my friend, Heribert Niehues, who took several of the photographs that are featured in the book on his trips through the wonderful United States! Thanks a lot Heribert, I appreciate your photographer's art.

Enjoy,

Bjoern Marek

Photo ©: Bjoern Marek, Heribert Niehues, Archive Bjoern Marek, Author photo on page 5, Peter Schulz.

Field of dreams

Parked alongside the historic Route 66 in particular, you'll always find some well-worth-seeing automobile relics from the glory days of transportation. In this case, we are talking about a Ford pickup, built in the thirties of the last century. It was parked and forgotten near the little town of Texola, in the state of Oklahoma. Although the winters here are hard, the sheet metal of the truck is in not-too-bad condition, but nearly all of the attached parts are gone, thanks to the many spares and souvenir hunters over the decades.

Forgotten luxury

Whilst the Interstate 40 bypasses the town of Canute in Oklahoma, the old US Highway 66 runs directly through the northern part of the small city. Here, this 1946 Cadillac is resting in peace.

17,100 four-door limousines were once built as Series 61 and Series 62, and you had to pay at least $2176 to make one your own. As an alternative, you could buy a two-door Club Coupe or a Convertible Coupe, but most customers chose to buy the four-door version, seen in this picture – the perfect upper-class family cruiser.

Under the hood, a straight-eight-cylinder engine of 346in³ waited to be fired-up, topped by a double-barrel carburetor made by Carter or Stromberg, and developing 150hp at 3400rpm which was transferred to the rear axle by a syncromesh manual transmission with three gears, or a Hydra-Matic automatic (plus $176). All Cadillacs from 1946 had enough power to handle the steeper mountain grades.

Customers often liked luxury equipment details like the automatic choke, foglamps, and the Safety Spotlight, controllable from the driver's seat.

Thunderbird relic

When the Corvette went on sale in 1953, General Motors had a product to catch potential customers that were originally interested in buying the compact sports roadsters made in Europe. Understandably, just two years later, the Ford Motor Company was trying to do the same by presenting its brand new model, the Thunderbird.

Like the Corvette, the first generation T-Bird also came in a simple package, with two seats and the perfect mix of elegance and sportiness. From the 1958 model year and onwards, the Thunderbird received a back seat – to appeal to more families and counteract slow sales figures. The plan succeeded, and 37,892 cars were sold in that model year – almost more than double the figure compared to 1957.

Seen here is a 1962 Thunderbird, of which 78,011 were sold. Most of them were built as a two-door Hardtop Coupe, and as an alternative, customers were able to get a Landau Hardtop with vinyl roof, a Convertible (9844 cars sold), or a Sports Roadster that was delivered with a fibreglass cover over the rear seats.

All T-Birds from 1962 were powered by a V8 of 390in³, optionally with 300 or 340 horses.

The car shown here is waiting to be 'reawakened' at the curbside of the US Highway 63, near Hardy in Arkansas.

Forgotten Mopar

In the city center of Crystal River, situated in the western part of Florida at the Gulf of Mexico, and well-known for providing the possibility of swimming with manatees, we find this 1964 Chrysler Newport, resting in peace.

Beneath the series 300 New Yorker and the 300K letter-series model, the Newport models were the cheapest way to own a Chrysler (from $2901). In total 85,183 Newports were sold in 1964, broken down into 55,957 four-door limousines, 10,579 two-door hardtop coupes, 9710 four-door limousines – without B-pillar; 3720 four-door Town & Country station wagons, and 2176 two-door convertibles. The standard engine was a V8 of 361in³ producing 265hp at 4400rpm.

The dealer introduction of the 1964 models was on September 20, 1963, a year in which a total of 145,192 cars left the Chrysler plants, making the company the eleventh biggest car manufacturer of that year.

Ghost

A reminder of the once glorious past of the Californian town of Bodie is this old rusty shell that was formerly a beautiful car from the 1920s. It fits perfectly between the wooden houses that decades ago illustrated the life force of the town, which in the 1880s had a population of nearly 8000 citizens.

Bodie is located in the eastern foothills of the Sierra Nevada Mountains, and was founded in 1859 by William S Body, who discovered gold in the region. Sixty-five saloons, a small Chinatown quarter, and hundreds of houses should have ensured the town's future, but unfortunately, just a few years after the town had reached its peak, the mines were empty, and by the beginning of World War II the last of the townsfolk had left this out-of-the-way area.

Nowadays, many of the deserted buildings still remind us of the town's interesting history – and that of its cars, like the one shown here.

Shrunken truck

This reinterpretation of a classic was found on the west coast of Florida, at the Gulf of Mexico. As a basis, the unknown owner used an old International Loadstar 1600 truck, which he put on a shorter chassis. This gives the whole composition a kind of cartoon-like look. However, it is nice to see that classics like these are still being used even today as workhorses, although the Floridian weather has affected the body of the truck, causing a lot of rust.

Lost Comet

Whilst a Ford was considered the entry-level to owning a car, it was Mercury that gave customers a higher and richer level of interior specification, and desirable features in general.

Here, a Mercury Comet from 1973 can be seen, waiting to be revitalised in Chiefland, Florida, along the North Highway 19, behind a Tire and Automotive Service station. The Comet was the base model of Mercury (beside Montego, Montego MX Brougham, Montego GT, Cougar, Cougar XR-7, Monterey, Monterey Custom, Marquis and Marquis Brougham), and could be ordered as a sedan model, with two or four doors. The car shown in the picture is one of the 55,707 two-door models built in 1973. A minimum price of $2432 was required in order to own one. It shared almost the same basic styling as its original design, when it was introduced in 1971.

The Comet had a wheelbase of 103in (two-door) or 109.9in (four-door), and was 185.4in or 192.3in in length. Both models were powered by a six-cylinder engine of 250in³ producing a tame 94hp at 3800rpm. At extra cost, you could get your Comet with one of two alternative engines: a 88hp version of the 250in³ six-cylinder or a V8 with 302in³, two-barrel carburetor and 138 horses.

Nearly 90 per cent of the Comets were ordered with radios and automatic transmissions, and 46 per cent had the V8 under their hood.

Firemen's favourite

The American LaFrance Company is one of the oldest manufacturers of fire trucks. It was founded in 1903, when it was then based in Elmira, New York. Over the decades, the company has built thousands of fire trucks, with aerial ladders, water pumps, or chemical engines.

Even today, American LaFrance trucks still have a classic design, like the ancient model shown here, parked behind an old building in the middle of Death Valley in California. The overall condition of the Fire Truck, with its open cabin, is good and nearly rust-free, due to the dry climate of the Mojave Desert; one of the driest, lowest, and hottest locations in North America.

Luxury beside the road

On the subject of the most beautiful Buicks of all time, the 1949 model year is a 'must-have.' This was the first year that the designers presented the Ventiports, a design feature that is incorporated into the front fenders – three per side for the Super models and four per side for the Roadmaster models. Nowadays, designers sometimes use this stylistic device to remind us of the glorious past of Buick.

Seen on here is a Super model from 1949. Only 5777 cars were built as a four-door limousine. They were powered by a straight-eight engine, of 320in³ and with a compression ratio of 6.9:1, which gave 150hp at 3600rpm. This car was parked alongside the US Highway 163, near Bluff, in Utah.

International workhorse

In January 1947, the International Harvester Company (IHC) introduced its latest truck series – the KB. As had been done by many other manufacturers, it was rather like an evolution of a design first used before World War II and, in IHC's case, was produced with only minor changes until the 1949 model year. Compared to 1946 models, the grille was higher and wider, and the hood emblem was attached to it. The windshield was still a two-piece affair as before, a design feature that didn't change until the 1950 model year.

As standard equipment, the IHC's cab featured, amongst other things, an 80mph speedometer, a water temperature gauge, a big bench-seat, and a glovebox. The chassis had solid front and rear axles, and motive power came from a Green Diamond straight-six-cylinder engine of 213in^3, with a single-barrel carburetor from Zenith, which produced 82hp at 3400rpm.

The pickup seen here is resting in peace near Adrian, in the state of Texas on the old Route 66.

Stylish ambulance

This ambulance, straight out of the 1950s, is parked behind a barn in the south-western part of Utah, which means that it is permanently exposed to wind and weather. Hidden in the snow, the second picture of this forgotten beauty was taken in November 2008, while the larger photo was taken in March of the same year.

The GMC trucks were available with different body layouts; for example, as a Suburban with side windows, seen here in these pictures, or alternatively as a pickup, with an open cargo area. They were all powered by a six-cylinder engine of 225in^3 and 100hp.

German duo

Besides the many pieces of American iron from long ago you will, of course, find some foreign vehicles as well, like Mercedes, driven mostly by people who 'brought home the bacon.' But alas, once they have reached the end of their life cycle, these vehicles must give way to a new car and are left forgotten in a parking lot, a barn, or a backyard.

These two nearly 40-year-old battered road cruisers from Germany brave all the weather God throws at them. They are parked on Highway 61, near Port Gibson, in the state of Louisiana, where the aggressive sun has bleached their paint.

Entry-level elegance

The Special-series was the entry-level for the potential Buick customer in 1954. The cars had received a fresh body style for the new model year; wider and lower in appearance, and a new panoramic windshield was used. Of course, the Ventiports were once again found on the front fenders, and these have been a typical design detail for Buick right up to the present day, as well as the chrome Sweepspear that runs down each side of the body from the front to the back of the car.

The car shown was found in Texola, Oklahoma, on the old Route 66, and is one of 70,356 four-door sedans from the Special-series, built in 1954. In addition to this body style, people could also buy their Buicks as a two-door Sedan, a two-door Hardtop Coupe, a two-door Convertible Coupe, and a four-door Station Wagon. In total, 190,884 Special models left the General Motors' plants in that year.

All versions were powered by an eight-cylinder engine of 264in^3 fitted with a Stromberg or Carter two-barrel carburetor and developing 143hp at 4200rpm (150hp when ordered with automatic transmission).

For the family

The VW Type 2, T1 or 'Bus' was the second model, after the Beetle, developed for civilian use by the Volkswagen Company. It was introduced to the German market on March 8, 1950, for a base price of 5850DM, and was manufactured up until 1967, when the T2 was introduced.

The T1 had a length of 4150mm, a width of 1606mm and a height of 1909mm, based on a wheelbase of 2400mm that it shared with the VW Beetle. Between 1950 and 1967 the T1 had several evolutions of its four-cylinder boxer engine, starting with a 1131cc engine with 25hp, a 1192cc engine with 30hp or 34hp, up to a 1493cc version with 42hp or 44hp at the end of the production cycle.

More than 1.8 million VW vans left the assembly lines in different body versions within the T1's lifetime. The T1 shown here is parked in a field beside the old Route 66 in Seligman, Arizona.

Forgotten four

There are four classics from the forties waiting to be brought back to life on the State Highway 96/old Route 66 near Avilla, in the state of Missouri. In the foreground, you can see a four-door Pontiac Sedan, built in the 1940 model year. This model was powered by a 223in^3 six-cylinder or a straight-eight, with 249in^3, both developing 100hp at 3800rpm.

The interior shot shows the inside of a Chevrolet Special Deluxe, built in 1941, also at this location.

Although this resting place has been largely forgotten over the years, there were still enough people passing by to steal some of the interior parts, whilst other parts have simply turned to dust.

Postwar premiere

World War II was not only a time of horror for humanity, but in many respects, for the car industry too. Many car manufacturing plants had to produce war machinery instead of civilian vehicles in order to meet the worldwide war demand. Luckily, this situation would change in 1945, a year which found the American population begging for new cars. However, there was a problem – while the war was going on, no car manufacturer was able to develop any new civilian products. The solution for many companies was to simply use their prewar models from 1942 as a basis for postwar models, and just overhaul them a bit. This happened to the 1946 two-door Ford Super Deluxe Sedan, seen in this picture that was pictured near Interior, on the State Highway 44 in South Dakota.

With 372,543 cars produced, the Super Deluxe series was the most popular Ford in 1946, and customers could choose between five different two-door bodies and two four-door versions.

The customer entry into the world of Ford vehicles was meant to be via the Deluxe models, with a base price of $1074, although the cheapest Super Deluxe could be bought for $1148. Both versions were powered by a 226in³ six-cylinder engine producing 90hp at 3300rpm. As an alternative, you could also buy your Ford with an eight-cylinder engine, bringing 239in³ and 100hp at 3800rpm.

A fallen meteor

While the Ford Motor Company offered vehicles at prices that allowed entry into the car market, in contrast, Mercury cars were more expensive, having more chrome and better base equipment, placing the company in the middle price sector, above Ford and below Lincoln.

The Mercury shown here is a 1962 Meteor Custom model, parked and forgotten along Old Route 66 near the town of Cuervo, in the state of New Mexico. The four-door Sedan was one of 23,484 cars built in the Meteor Custom-series, where a tarting price of $2428 was required to call it your own. The mid-sized Meteor shared the same basic body as the Ford Fairlane, but used more styling details from the bigger Mercury models. The Custom model featured more chrome trim than the base Meteor, e.g. on the side windows, lower rear quarter panels, roof, side and rocker panels. It had a wheelbase of 116.5in and was approximately 204in in length. All Meteors were powered as standard by a 170in^3 six-cylinder engine, topped by a Holley single-barrel carburetor and with a power output of 101hp at 4400rpm. You could also order your Meteor with a 221in^3 V8 (145hp) or a 260in^3 V8 with 164hp. Only 17 per cent of the 1962 Mercurys were ordered with a six-cylinder engine.

Old giant

The F-series from 1948 was the first really new postwar development truck, and was different from the previous model year through its new one-piece windshield, squared-off fenders, redesigned front with its new recessed grille (including horizontal bars) and the headlights.

The cab received the new 'million dollar design,' and was longer, taller and wider than ever before, giving more room for passengers. There was also less vibration, due to the presence of new rubber parts separating the cab from the chassis.

The 1949 F-Series was separated into F-1, F-2, F-3 and F-4, while the truck shown on the picture belongs to the biggest, Heavy-Duty-series from 1949. This Ford is waiting to be rediscovered and renovated in Cuervo, New Mexico on the old Route 66.

Big hauler

Consolidated Freightways, today known as Freightliner, was founded in the 1930s. It now belongs to Daimler Trucks North America LLC, and is the largest heavy-duty truck manufacturer in the northern United States.

In the beginning, it produced modified trucks, based on Fageols, by installing more powerful engines to enable its customers to better handle the steep gradients in the mountains. These trucks had "Freightliner" emblems on the body.

The overgrown 'workhorse' in the picture was built in the 1970s, and can be seen in a field near the town of Wakefield in Louisiana, on US Highway 61. Rest in peace, faithful servant.

Nature is calling

It's always impressive to see what a short amount of time it takes for nature to recapture the fabrications of mankind. Like these cars, created in the '70s and '80s to serve their human masters, then parked and forgotten years ago on grassland, beside a rickety old barn.

This trio, and their companion at the back, wait to be rediscovered and reawakened on US Highway 41A in the town of Shelbyville, located in Tennessee in the south-eastern United States.

Family truck

Amongst the trucks most loved by enthusiasts is the Chevrolet Suburban from the 1950s. This classic is parked on State Highway 110, in Silverton, Colorado, and was built in the 1954 model year. It used the half-ton commercial platform, and was the most expensive body version of the 3100 series (starting from $1958). Buyers could choose between two doors (as here, designated 3106), or a tailgate at the back (designated 3116). Despite being a Suburban model, the 3100 series included the following body versions: chassis and cowl, chassis and cab, pickup, panel delivery and canopy.

The 1954 Suburban had a wheelbase of 116in, was 195.3in long and had a height of 79.5in. Power was provided by an in-line six-cylinder engine, with a Rochester single-barrel carburetor, producing 105hp at 3600rpm.

Apache pickup

Like its smaller siblings, the 1959 Chevrolet Apache 3600 pickup featured the new Task Force design with its panoramic windshield and windshield pillars raked to the front, quad front headlights (introduced in the previous model year), and a grille with a massive-looking central bar. The edges of the grille carried turn signal lights of oval design.

Running across the front of the hood, 1959 models wore a big Chevrolet 'Bowtie'; while you could find the model identification – in the case of the truck on this picture, a Chevrolet Apache 36 – on the front fenders.

To give both commercial and private customers the chance to individualise their trucks, new Apaches could be bought in a variety of colours that were once limited to use on Chevrolet cars. Now buyers were able to choose Baltic Blue, Sherwood Green, Omaha Orange, Tartan Turqouise, Yukon Yellow or even Pure White.

Group picture of the generations

The classic car on the right of this picture is one of the legendary 'Tri-Chevys', meaning the cars that were built between the 1955 and 1957 model years. Nowadays, especially, worldwide car collectors love the elegant two-door Bel Air hardtop coupes, as well as the four-door sedan of the Two-Ten-series from 1957, shown here. A beauty that's for sure, although wind and weather has bleached its paint. In 1957, 260,401 Two-Ten models were produced. However, it was particularly the two-tone paint schemes – available for the One-Fifty, Two-Ten and Bel Air-series – that emphasized the body lines.

The car parked beside the Chevrolet is a 1964 Ford Galaxie 500. The two-door sedan, shown here, could be ordered with six-cylinder engines, but most customers chose a V8 for their car (with prices starting at $2613).

Hay transporter

One of the main economic forces in the early history of the United States was the agricultural industry, which needed a good and reliable means of transportation in order to bring tools from the farm to the field; vegetables to the farmers' market, or hay back to the barn.

We discovered this truck in a little town on our way to Arizona's Grand Canyon, about an hour after passing the great Hoover Dam. We left the highway at the Chloride Billboard, and drove all the way up to the little touristic ghost town of Chloride. It's situated in Mohave County, and has its beginnings in the early 1860s. Back then, silver chloride (as well as other metals like lead, copper or zinc) had been discovered at the site, giving the town its name. In 1944, during World War II, the cost of extracting the ore rose, and manpower was in short supply; consequently, the mining stopped. Today, you can still see some original wooden buildings from Chloride's heyday, when about 2000 people lived there – as well as, of course, this wonderful old truck.

Classic duo

Here are two cars not seen too often at car meetings worldwide. The rarest is the unusually designed Nash Rambler, to the left of the picture. It's one of 25,785 two-door coupes produced, which were first offered for sale to the public on April 1, 1952. The base price for the car on its wheelbase of 100in, with a total length of 176in, was $2094. The Rambler featured an in-line six-cylinder engine with a displacement of 172.6in³, a Carter single-barrel carburetor, and 82hp at 3800rpm on tap. The Nash Motor Company celebrated its 50th Anniversary in 1952, a year when 152,141 cars where produced, giving Nash an American market share of 3.51 per cent.

The classic on the right was built in 1942 by Oldsmobile. It's a Club Coupé that was first presented to the public with the other Olds models on August 29th 1941. The reason these cars went on sale much earlier in this year than previous years was because Oldsmobile (like most manufacturers) would be required to reduce civilian car production in the near future, as advised by the War Production Board, and shift to producing military machinery for World War II.

All models received a visual makeover with a new front grille, double-duty bumpers, and new pontoon-style fender design all around. Under the hood, an in-line six-cylinder engine of 238in³, with a single-barrel carburetor producing 100hp at 3200rpm was fitted as standard. Power was transmitted to the rear wheels by a three-speed manual gearbox, or a Hydra-Matic automatic, with four speeds: the latter could also be combined with an in-line eight-cylinder with 257in³ developing 110 horses.

Historic stop

The General Store in Hackberry, Arizona, is a combination of an old gas station, disused these days, and a memorabilia store for Route 66 items – definitely a 'must-do' stop for tourists and fans travelling along the historic east-west highway.

Despite possibly needing some ice cream or a cold soda to cool down, it's always nice to roam between the classic cars and truck relics, found on and around the site. These two classics from the 1930s, for example, are resting in the Arizonian sun and maybe dreaming of a rebirth that might never come. But apart from this, there's more to see, like a Ford Model T flatbed truck in a classic service garage; old gas pumps and signs, and even a nicely restored red and white 1957 Corvette which is often parked in front of the store.

Prewar truck

Most noticeably, the 1941 models of the Chevrolet light-duty trucks differed from previous models because of their new, bold grille design (they're now called the 'Waterfall-Chevy' by many enthusiasts). For 41 the headlights were placed in the fenders, instead of being mounted beside the grille. Compared to 1940, the wheelbase had grown from 113 to 115in, although the six-cylinder engine of its 216.5in^3 stayed nearly the same, it now produced 90hp at 3300rpm, with a Carter single-barrel carburetor sitting on the top.

The Light-Duty model 'AK', seen here on State Highway 90, near the town of Bedrock in Colorado, could be ordered in several versions: chassis only ($478), chassis and cabin ($569), pickup ($600), panel ($686), canopy ($722) and, as a Suburban model ($837). The trucks were introduced in September 1940, and 212,797 units were produced in the 1941 model year alone.

School's out

Near the city of Glenwood, in the state of New Mexico, this school bus is resting in peace beside the US Highway 180. It seems to be a model from the early 1940s that was parked here a long time ago. All the glass is gone, as are the headlights and most of the interior. However, couldn't you still imagine bringing the old bus back to life, cruising from classic car show to classic car show, and getting many 'thumbs-ups' and trophies? Never say never … Maybe this bus' time will come again, through an enthusiast falling in love with this piece of old, but nostalgia packed, American iron.

Route 66 commemoration

The General Store in Hackberry, Arizona, is one of the few scenes along the legendary Route 66 where the spirit of that glorious road has survived up until the present day.

Far from the new Interstate 40, which has by-passed, and so caused the demise of small towns along the Old Route 66 (although it runs parallel, it was built at some distance from this historic east-west connection) you'll find a revitalised piece of history. The General Store features contemporary gas pumps and hundreds of pieces of Route 66 memorabilia that help keep the famous road's spirit alive. Joining this scene are several classic cars and trucks in varying conditions that are scattered about the area. One of these cars is this 1930 Ford Model A that, in combination with the shack in the background, delivers a nearly perfect photo scene.

The Model A was the replacement for the Model T, with which Henry Ford started the mass-production of the automobile. Between 1928 and 1931 more than five million Model A Fords left the production plants – an impressive number, and one about which the automobile manufacturers of today can only dream.

Ghost town relic

If you want to see a real ghost town in beautiful condition, Bodie is the place to go. Situated east of the Sierra Nevada Mountains in Central California, Bodie was originally founded in 1861, and accommodated in its heyday more than 10,000 citizens, who enjoyed life in the 65 saloons and amusement arcades. Today, the town consists of about 200 remains of buildings that act as a reminder of its golden age.

Scattered around the city limits you can find several cars in pretty poor condition. One of the highlights is this Chevrolet, built in the 1937 model year. About 20,000 of these two-door coupes once left the plants, all of them powered by a six-cylinder-engine of 85hp.

Super Sedan

Exactly 10,000 of the Super four-door sedans left the Buick plants in the 1951 model year. In contrast to the base-series Special the Super models had a longer body, but featured almost the same overall design as their siblings.

With great attention to detail, the Ventiports on the side of the front fenders were the typical design feature that told everyone 'here comes a Buick.' Specials and Supers had three of these vents in their fenders, and the top model Roadmaster displayed four. The turn signal lights, with their chrome-bezels, were situated each side of the grille with its vertical bars. The side view of the 1951 Buick was accentuated with a curved chrome 'spear.'

You could buy your 1951 Buick Super model for a base price of $2248 (as a two-door Super Sedanette), the four-door Station Wagon was the most expensive way to own a Super model (starting at $3133). This might also be the reason why relatively few family cruisers were sold.

Pickup mania

The 1948 F-1 model was Ford's first new truck development after World War II. Five horizontal bars define the grille that, in the case of the pictured half-ton pickup, is hiding behind an extra metal guard. In contrast to the previous year the F-1 now featured a one-piece windshield and wider fenders that gave the truck the perfect mix of modernity and robustness.

The driver's cabin, billed as the "million-dollar cab" is longer, wider, and has more head clearance than the models from 1947, and is also much better protected from vibration and exterior noise, thanks to the recent installation of rubber pads between chassis and cab. Business and private customers could order their F-1 from January 26, 1948 in several different configurations besides the typical pickup bed, also as a chassis cab.

Divided into the four series F-1 to F-4, 143,000 trucks were built in the 1948 model year, the best year for sales since 1929.

Fine Forties

As with nearly all other car manufacturers, Chevrolet also presented a warmed-over version of its 1942 prewar model to get its market share of the pent-up demand after World War II. The 1946 to 1948 model year ranges consisted of prewar models, as the company did not show its new postwar design until 1949.

Here, you can see a Chevrolet from the Fleetmaster-series produced in the 1948 model year. It is parked near Mammoth Spring in Arkansas, on US Highway 63. In 1948, the company divided its cars into two series: the Stylemaster – the model that allowed entry into Chevy-world – and the Fleetmaster, the upmarket version. There were several differences between the two: for example, the use of more chrome on the body and around the windshield, a two-spoke deluxe steering wheel, leather-topped front seat armrests, and a wood-grained dashboard for the Fleetmaster.

Of the four-door sedans, as seen here, 93,142 were produced as a 1948 model (base price was $1439), but you could also get your 'Chevy' as a two-door Town Sedan ($1381), two-door Sport Coupe ($1402), two-door Convertible ($1750), and four-door Station Wagon ($2013). The sub-series Fleetline consisted of a four-door Master Sedan ($1492) and a two-door Aero Sedan ($1434). In total, Chevrolet produced 775,982 units in the 1948 model year.

All cars came with a wheelbase of 116in, used 16-inch tires and featured a six-cylinder engine of 216.5in^3, delivering 90hp at 3300rpm. A three-speed manual was the only choice of transmission.

Back to the Eighties

Oldsmobile was a car manufacturing company with a long history. It was founded in 1897 by Randon E Olds, and sold millions of cars, mostly in latter years when it was in the ownership of General Motors. Oldsmobile has, however, been defunct since 2004.

One of the most popular models of Oldsmobile was the 88-series. This full-size model existed from 1949 until 1999, and was an image-builder for the whole company when introduced with its powerful V8, dropped into a light-weight chassis, ready to enter the world of motor racing. Up until 1999, when it was discontinued, there were eleven generations of the 88 model. Here in a photo taken in Newcastle, Utah, on State Highway 56, you can see a car produced in Generation 9 between 1977 and 1985. Back then, you were able to order your 88 as a two-door coupe or four-door sedan, powered by one of five engines: a V6 of 231in^3, or three-gasoline V8s displacing 305, 350 or 403in^3. A diesel V8 with 350in^3 was also available, and as with the other engine options, always combined with one of two versions of a three-speed automatic (TH200 or TH350), or a four-speed automatic called THM-200-4R.

Studebaker graveyard

At the beginning of 1852, a European immigrant family named Studebaker started a business in the United States building horse-drawn carriages. By the beginning of the 20th century, the company was getting ready for the construction and the selling of automobiles. Only three decades later, the Studebaker Company had grown into one of the bigger car manufacturers in the US. However, the business closed down in 1966, primarily because of mistakes made in its marketing policy.

Cars, like the ones in these pictures, were built in the heyday of the Studebaker Corporation, especially the two relics on the right – officially called "Starlight Coupes" – they were cars that polarised the masses. Interestingly, the rear window portion of the cars, as seen from the outside, reminded many people of an aircraft cockpit.

The blue, restored classic seen below is a 1949 Champion Regal Deluxe two-door Starlight Coupe. It's powered by an in-line six-cylinder engine of 170in³, with a Carter single-barrel carburetor, and producing 80hp at 4000rpm. The Starlight is 192.5in long and has a wheelbase of 112in. In 1949, 9829 Starlight Coupés were built, and a base price of $1757 was required in order to call one your own. This classic is proudly owned by the author of this book, and is regularly driven around the streets of his hometown in Germany.

Old survivor

This more-than-six-decades-old classic is rusting in peace near Avilla in the state of Missouri near the old Route 66. We are talking about a Buick Eight, one built for the 1941 model year. Five series were sold: Special, Super, Century, Roadmaster and Limited. The wheelbase was different for nearly each series. The Special was sold on a chassis with 118 or 121in wheelbase, while the Super could only be ordered with a 121-inch chassis. The Century and the Roadmaster shared a platform with a 126in wheelbase, while the Limited series had a larger 139-inch platform.

The engine choices were much simpler: Specials and Supers featured a straight-eight-cylinder of 248in^3, whilst the Centurys, Roadmasters and Limiteds were powered by a 320in^3 version. You can differentiate the Specials and Supers from their bigger brothers by simply checking the vents and the curve on the front fender. The smaller series only had four vents instead of five, and the curve of the fender ran nearly up to the front door, instead of having a flat piece of bodywork between the door and the the fender.

Rusty companion

Here we can see a Ford Super Deluxe, first shown to the public on October 22, 1945, and built in this design between 1946 and 1948. Ford divided its models into the two series Deluxe and Super Deluxe, for which a six-cylinder engine of 226in^3, with a single-barrel carburetor from Holley, producing 90hp at 3300rpm, was the base engine. Optionally, you could order your Ford with an eight-cylinder engine of 239in^3, with a Holley two-barrel carburetor and 100hp at 3800rpm on tap. This car was painted by one of its owners to look like an old Highway Patrol car.

Studebaker's workhorse

After the end of World War II Studebaker, like other companies went back to producing civilian vehicles. Its first creation was the M5 pickup, seen here in Glenwood, New Mexico, on US Highway 180. Because it was unable to develop any new products during the war, Studebaker, as with other car manufacturers, used its prewar model from 1941 with slight modifications. Whilst many previous options like two windshield wipers, an oil filter, a dome light and armrests now came as standard. Strangely, it came with a spare wheel, but the 16-inch tire for it was missing; the reason being that there was a shortage of tires after the end of the war.

In the 1946 model year, Studebaker built 14,052 of its M5 trucks, the base price being $929. All pickups were equipped with a six-cylinder engine of 169.6in^3, featuring a Carter single-barrel carburetor and an oil bath air cleaner: power output was 80hp at 4000rpm.

Postwar child

Shortly after the end of World War II most car manufacturers started to produce civilian vehicles once more. Eager to get back to normal life, there was a big demand from the public for new cars and other technological goods. Buick – handicapped by the war effort, and therefore like other manufacturers, not able to develop a totally new car – refreshed its 1942 models slightly, in order to make them quickly available to the postwar market.

Seen here is a Buick built in 1946, and located in Springerville in the state of Arizona on US Highway 191. The Buick portfolio that year consisted of three different series – the Specials, the Supers and the Roadmasters. Cars could be ordered as four-door sedans (the Special from $1580, the Super from $1822, the Roadmaster from $2110); Station Wagons (the Super from $2594); two-door Sedanettes (the Special from $1522, the Super from $1741, the Roadmaster: from $2014) and two-door convertible coupes (the Super from $2046, the Roadmaster from $2347).

All cars were powered by an in-line engine with eight cylinders, using a two-barrel carburetor from Stromberg or Carter and producing 144hp at 3600rpm. A manual transmission with three gears was standard, and the only option.

Eager beaver

If you are going along the US Highway 385 near Hemingford, in the state of Nebraska, you might see this International pickup hiding in a field. It's one of the KB-3-series built between 1947 and 1949, and this identification is confirmed by looking at the lettering used on the body in front of the doors under the International lettering on the sides of the hood. Beside the KB-1 and KB-2, the truck version shown here was the biggest series available from International Harvester Company (IHC). It looked similar to its smaller brothers, but came with heavier running gear and larger tires. It could be bought as a chassis only, chassis and cowl, Express pickup, KM (Milk Transporter), panel van or stake side.

All trucks were powered by the same 213in^3 Green Diamond engine with six-cylinders, a Zenith single-barrel carburetor, producing 82hp at 3400rpm. Between 1947 and 1949 43,0351 IHC trucks left the assembly lines, and approximately 15,000 people worked at the IHC headquarters in Chicago, Illinois.

Batwings

In 1958 the nomenclature "Impala" was at first an upgrade package for the Chevrolet Bel Air models, but one year later it had become a series in its own right. You could buy your Impala as a two-door Hardtop, Convertible or Coupe, or as a four-door version with or without B-pillar. One of the four-door hardtop sedans can be seen on this picture, taken beside Highway 90, near the town of Marathon in the state of Texas.

The base engine of the 1959 Impalas (with a starting price of $2592) was a Blue Flame straight-six-cylinder of 235in³, developing 135hp at 4000rpm. Optionally, there was a Turbo Fire V8 of 283in³ and 185hp at 4600rpm, or a Turbo Thrust V8 with 348in³ and 250hp at 4400rpm.

The key distinguishing features of a Chevrolet model from 1959 are definitely the 'Batwings', the nearly horizontal tail-fins at the rear of this full-size classic.

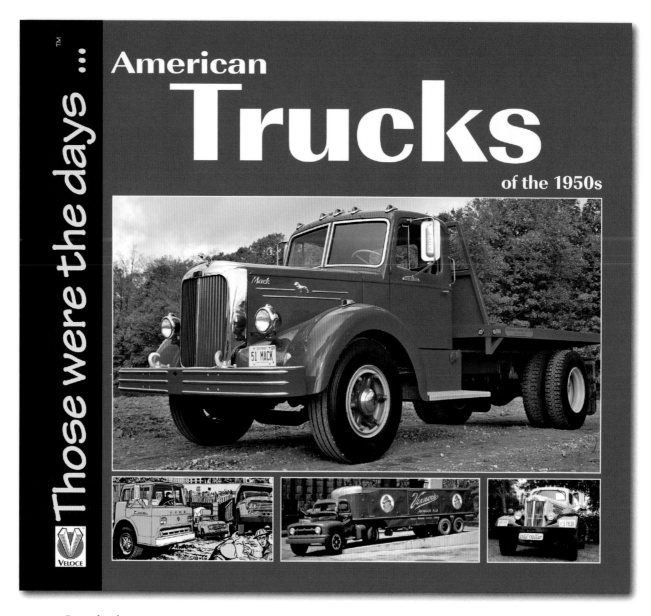

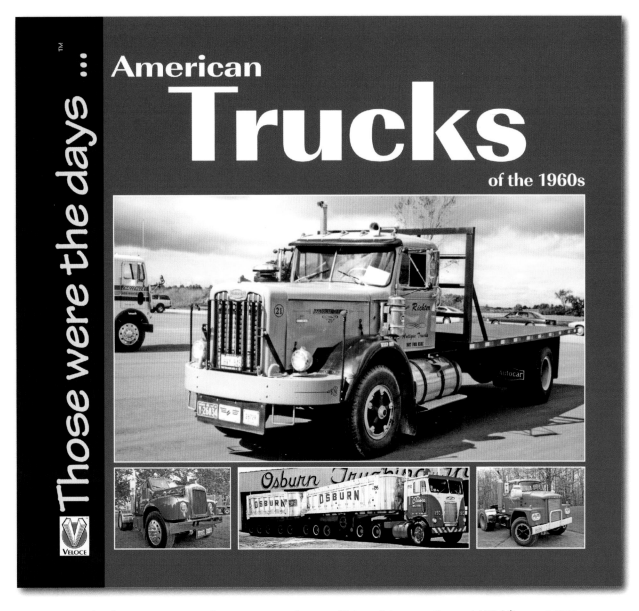

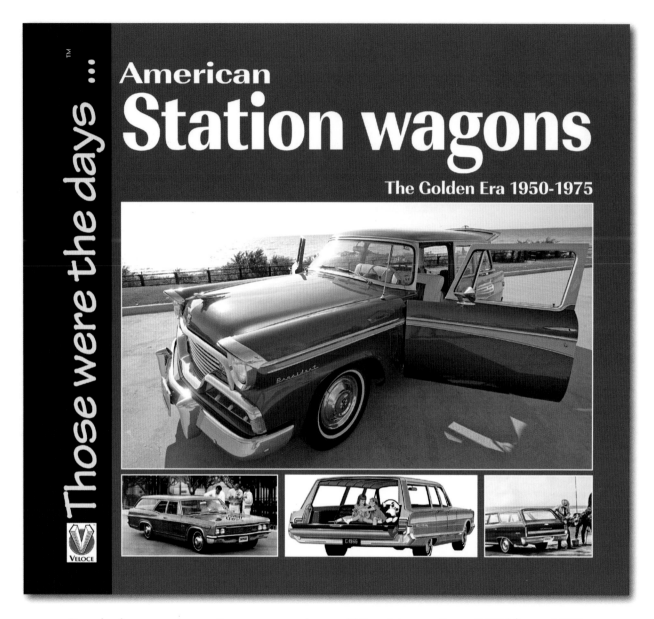

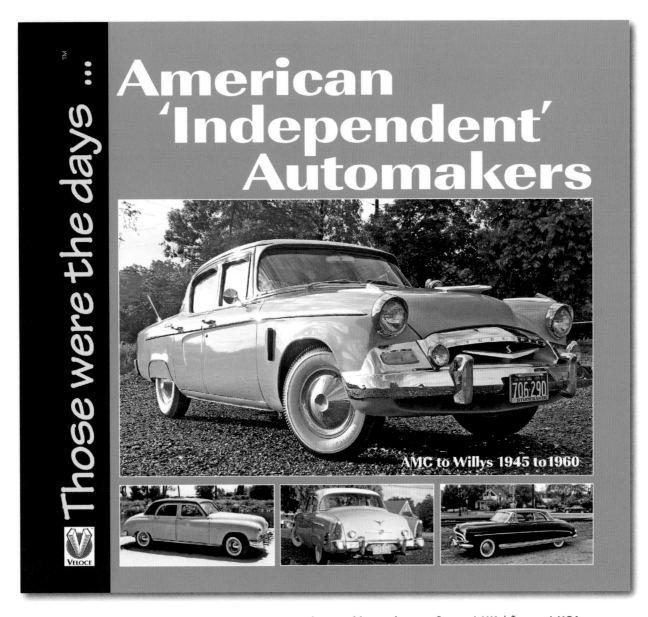

Index

American LaFrance 24, 25

Buick 26, 27, 34, 35, 70, 71, 80, 81, 86, 87

Cadillac 8, 9
Chevrolet 39, 50, 51-55, 62, 63, 68, 69, 74, 75, 90
Chrysler 12

Ford 6, 7, 10, 11, 14, 15, 20, 21, 40, 41, 44, 45, 54, 55, 60, 61, 66, 67,
    72, 73, 82, 83
Freightliner 46, 47

GMC 30, 31

International/IHC 16, 17, 28, 29, 88, 89

Mercedes 32, 33
Mercury 22, 23, 42, 43

Nash 58, 59

Oldsmobile 58, 59, 76, 77

Plymouth 18, 19
Pontiac 38, 39

Studebaker 78, 79, 84, 85

Volkswagen 36, 37